Hello, De-Realized me...

Ben C.G. Moore

BookLeaf Publishing

Presentation by *BookLeaf Publishing*

Web: www.bookleafpub.com

E-mail: info@bookleafpub.com

ISBN: 9789395784320

First edition 2022

DEDICATION

Lise St-Denis (Mom) and Charles-Guy St-Denis (Grand-papa), I miss you both. Thank you for showing me what's beyond that horizon...

ACKNOWLEDGEMENT

To my family, thanks for sticking by me. Even if at times, it seems that I make it harder than it has to be. And Bookleaf Publishing, for giving me this opportunity.

Animus liber

I never accepted "born this way" as a valid
claim.
Even if for most of it, it was done out of
necessity.
It is a choice, pure and simple; even if
self-evident.
And when I speak of choice, I evoke the will
of agency.
But to regress now means to bury yourself
back to what was before.
So, take it and embrace the path of life that
you have chosen for yourself.
For you are no more, no less than.
And never let anyone tell you otherwise.
Not even me…

One’s wounds

It seems that a man’s wound, just takes one to open many. This wound is a plague for the peace and harmony within. That few know its destructive power.

I’ve seen how it strikes in every different way. From anger to lust, crystalizing your heart; consuming the body and mind as well. It takes you into the darkest places that you can find.

Cold by flesh and blood, you`re the unstable weight that pushes the world down. Without even having the right conscience in control.

I’ve seen everything, everything that I needed to know how it is. And sometimes; a lot of times, I feel like this is something that I shouldn't know.

The Big Old Blue

Woke up in the Morning,
See the big old blue,
By the Window,
Everything could blow.

If I could have a boat,
I could run away,
See my friends again,
Where I can stay.

It sucks so bad,
To be alone,
In the middle of nowhere,
By the big old Blue.

If I make a boat,
I'll run away,
Meet my friends again,
Where I can stay.

Time

What is of the ancient, the old, modern and the new?
Drifts of time that goes by, to us the condemned.
Like looking at the universe from above.

And because we were damned from the start.
We treasure time as a shared value while it's present.
Till God decides that our time has passed.

For me, history is a growing wonder.
Thinking if we learned from the past
To relieve the burden of the next

I weep in vain to know tomorrow.
Either I want it or not; I, a mortal soul.
Passing on the torch to another, someday.

Art

It seems that legend tells every man has his
art.
It's what we all have, it defines our own
individuality.
For me, I have a way to imagine and create,
yet not by skill.
Therefore, I use it on something that already
exists.

Using my talent and knowledge.
My passion for words comes easy to mind.
Then, turning it into something new.
Yet it is for naught without heart and soul.

And this is for everybody that reads this.
So, the thing is when you want to do
something; just do it.
Treasure your dream and stop at nothing to
make it.
Cause the world won't do it for you.

Mein jungfrau

Hello old friend, fancy meeting you here,
Warden of my woes.
I wonder how many of my demons I've sent
to your cold embrace.
Yet, time and time again, you are a
monument to my torment and salvation.
For even if your siren's call tempts me, it
reminds me just how easy that would be.
But in this rain, I know you'd stave your
hand for now, though you keep watch in my
shadow. And so, I accept my fate as a man
half-dead, aimlessly walking the ends of the
earth, seeking Nirvana.
So, might as well get comfortable; for
there's a long journey ahead still, My lady.
Besides, I wonder what would tomorrow
bring…

The Highway Church

I am alpha and omega.
I am the shepherd that ever guards his flock.
And my conscience is your guide.
But like any other deity, I don't spare any
who strays on the path.
Yet I owe my existence to your need to
bridge worlds.

Either to the south or north, trail from the
east to west, then back again.
Some call me the angel of freedom; others,
the tyrannical king of your boredom.
Whenever, night or day, the door to my
congregation is always open.
No matter how you wish to wander, all
believe in me.
For the journey is what I preach.

And whenever you decide to leave for higher pastures.
I will be waiting, ready to welcome you again with open arms.
All I ask is that you never forget your reasons for being on the path.
From your destination and to your fellow man, whom you travel with.
And as we must part once more, I bid you fare thee well...

Sins of the father, atonement of the son

The seeds of progress that had once been established.
Now grown out of range of our knowledge.
So here we are, in this sludge of toxic orange.
Left by our ancestors, in which the issue remained in storage.

As they plundered and the soil slowly withered.
Their reason to carry on was for Gold and Silver.
As they said, "All hail the almighty dollar".
Would they say the same, if this was now their future?

But I reminisce as the past cannot be altered.
And as this tale will be told till my skin turns purple.
Pray to never forget this lesson, my dear pupil.
As you become the keeper of Gaia and its people.

Lament of the horizon

If I were younger,
Stronger,
Faster,
Smarter,
Wiser,

Would I be bolder and happier than I am;
with the shackles that now bind me?

Amet amor

Have you ever had a strange feeling about someone?
Like your face is blushed all over,
And your heart boils like magma,
Well for me, I've seen it countless times.
But barely for myself.

At first, it comes with being ecstatic and the promise of social status.
But as the Wiseman said, “beauty is only skin deep”,
By the time you admitted that you were wrong,
You eventually start acknowledging his words of wisdom,
But it isn’t something to change,

Because this is how you find your first love.

Satiating rain

We all aspire for a better world before it's our turn to go below.
But for all the crusades and victories we amassed as a whole,
And the will of your forebears fulfilled, a query must be asked, though:

When the time comes, will you be willing to let go?

For fate may make you a monster worse than the one you fought to alleviate your woes. Then again, I'm just an old man slow at acknowledging this changing world is not my tomorrow.

Glory is for the dead

A warning to the young, who are eager.
A sermon & promise from those who lived it.
A reminder for jar-heads in the chaos of battle.
And a prayer, for the first line to cross over no man's land.

With the solemn pledge that we will remember them...

Martyrs of peace

You once said that those who lack ambition should be eliminated, and the weak should be destroyed. Gaze upon the fruits of your labor, thy conqueror. The melancholy of steel, blood and ash! The only refuge this world where you feel alive. So, I ask you what then? What you offer is change for good or ill; however just like a storm, it'll sooner or later subside, and the calm will take its place. And what shall become of thee? A mere spectre of a being you once were; if fate spared itself a Stonehenge from you.

You spend your days lamenting that the world's problems are but a grinding cycle into which we must adapt or die. True, we are all ants under a rock; as feeble as we are, however, we pull strength in numbers. And to that end, you wholeheartedly acknowledge that you have no place in this world…

Living the day, by the day

It's amazing how people think themselves as Gods
But for those who wear the uniform, it's a game
against all odds.

They who serve, they who sweat
They who come, they who go
Not knowing if they'll be here tomorrow.

It's amazing how people think themselves as Gods
But for those who wear the uniform, it's a game
against all odds.

For us who stayed, for us who are free
For us who love living, for us who don't share
Haven't we all learned?

It's amazing how people think themselves as Gods
But for those who wear the uniform, it's a game
against all odds.

As the sun rises, as the sun falls
As they come, as they go
They always say: to live the day, by the day.

Oculis in heptade

In this world, there is the pride of noble,
With the greed of impatience,
To the lust of the desired,
Into gluttony of pain for power,
The slothing end caused by ignorance,
The thrilling envy from agony,
And the wrath of endless vengeance.

Olá Saudade e a gente se vê

Forgive me my Lady, for I have sinned. What is thy transgression you may ask? As your patron, in my heart of hearts, I unwittingly may have asked of you to grant me "special privileges" upon your dealings. Upon this, is the greatest taboo of all; and for this travesty, I give you my deepest and sincerest apologies.

To me, you represent everything that could be, can be, that I want it to be. And even if to you, our moment was brief, you gave me heaven; leaving me with a debt that I could never repay. But I know that I can not truly give you what you want; curse this cage of mine and these chains that bind me to my torment.

But does this give me the right to damn you to the nine pits of hell, just to soothe my agony? No, I treasure the blissful moment we shared under the stars. Never to squander the joy you have gifted me; a crippled fool who like Icarus, wished to fly too close to the sun.

But I am but a mortal man, and I know that at any moment, the seven sins may take hold of me. Therefore, I will aspire to be half the man you believe me to be and set you free. At least by doing so l hope that, unlike Hades, I would prove to the world that I do not wish to be your jailor. So, fly away and live your life to your heart's content, my lover, my queen, my Valkyrie.

As for me, I'll stay here in this Inferno. Maybe someone else would come along and give me the deliverance I truly wish for, maybe. Until then, I shall wait, as always; and at least I'll cherish those pleasant memories. And by the time the void takes me, will it matter? Although there is one thing I do know for certain; like Atlas and Prometheus before me, I shall endure…

<u>Existential karma</u>

"You have the watches. We have the time..."
-Taliban Proverb

Then in the name of all Humankind,
I sentence you to eternal consternation,
Chasing your shadow with every step you take,
Knowing that what you offer is stagnation,
The people will make their own fate.
It may not come today, nor tomorrow, but
someday.

Spes occidere

"I don't want revenge on the Taliban, I want education for sons and daughters of the Taliban." — Malala Yousafzai

You pride yourself upon being the graveyard of empires.
Yet if you stay on your current course, that's all you'll ever be.
And even if from the surface, the law of "might makes right" is in play.
The key to prosperous longevity, is to forge lasting bonds with whom you live among this wide universe.

And at present, all you have are feeble and fragile alliances at best.
"Mere good governance is not enough; it has to be pro-people and pro-active.
Good governance is putting people at the center of development process." As they say. While it be a long climb to come back from the stumbles from our own hypocrisy. Why not rise to the occasion and give back for a change?

Either way, the world is watching…

Life’s question

Where do we come from?
And what are we for?
Haven’t you wondered before?
All I know is answers go as they come.

If it is so, let it go.
What will reveal tomorrow?
I guess we’ll never know.

As I ask myself who are we?
What is our life’s task?
What will we do till we gasp our last?
Some say this is how God meant us to be.

If it is so, let it go.
What will reveal tomorrow?
I guess we’ll never know.

I ask why and who will answer my call?
Where must I go even if I search high and dry?
Is it something destiny denies?
If so then it will be a hell of a fall.

If it is so, let it go.
What will reveal tomorrow?
I guess we’ll never know.

The unrequited door

I've been wanting to apologize to you for some time. About how I treated the connection that we had, you and me, through my posturing vanity, peaceable timing, or narcissistic pride. Either that you were of the same mind as my buried sentiments or just wanted to have some fun. Also, I wasn't sure how to approach the situation, given that I'm not someone you notice at first glance in said context. And in the end, I was a coward who just wanted to avoid embarrassment at all costs. Furthermore, I dreaded my daydreams of your affection with the sense I wouldn't reach the standard of expectations. Then again, it might have been destined to be this way regardless.

In truth, I miss you; but my golden opportunity once so disposable, has long passed. I hope that you have found what you are looking for and that you are happy. If not, I'll cheer you on even if I'll remain as a fragment of pleasant memories gone by. Best wishes to you, past, present, and future, who ever so briefly brighten my world. And who knows, maybe there's happiness yet to be found for me too.
Take care…

Human experience

Joy, thankfulness, and fellowship.
Pain, suffering and sorrow.
We have all these things.
And for most, it maws at us when one
extreme is nurtured over the other.
But it is easy when looking at the world
in hindsight.
And what was, is or could have been; are
only in hopeful thoughts.
In the end, all we can do is empathize,
for it to not occur next time around.
Although for some, it is inevitable that
the former is fated for repetition.
So, I ask thee, bound by the infinite
wheel of time.
Remember to be human.
With all its flaws and wonder.
May you find home.

"We are all visitors to this time, this place. We are just passing through. Our purpose here is to observe, to learn, to grow, to love… and then we return home" - Australian Aboriginal proverb

www.ingramcontent.com/pod-product-compliance
Lightning Source LLC
Chambersburg PA
CBHW051717130826
49812CB00034B/1227
* 9 7 8 9 3 9 5 7 8 4 3 2 0 *